DEVELOPING GENDER EQUALITY AND SOCIAL INCLUSION STRATEGIES FOR SECTOR AGENCIES IN SOUTH ASIA

A GUIDANCE NOTE

AUGUST 2023

ASIAN DEVELOPMENT BANK

ADB

Note:
In this publication, "$" refers to United States dollars.

On the cover: Villagers from Bharabhid village, Bajhang District, Nepal, are some of the Building Climate Resilience of Watersheds beneficiaries in the Mountain Eco-Regions Project (photo by Gerhard Jones).

Cover design by Josef Ilumin.

Contents

Tables and Box

Abbreviations

ADB	Asian Development Bank
GESI	gender equality and social inclusion
M&E	monitoring and evaluation
SARD	South Asia Department
SOGIESC	sexual orientation, gender identity and expression, and sex characteristics
ToC	theory of change

CHAPTER 1
Introduction

A.   Purpose of This Guidance Note

This guidance note provides the principles, approaches, and key points to consider in developing and operationalizing a government sector agency's gender equality and social inclusion (GESI) strategy.[1] The overall objective is to support sector agencies across the developing member countries of the South Asia Department (SARD) of the Asian Development Bank (ADB) to create an informed strategy for integrating GESI into their operations and institutions (i.e., policies, systems, and structures). The GESI strategy is expected to help the sector agency respond to sector-related barriers to GESI experienced by women and excluded and vulnerable groups. As the prevalent social and gender norms and practices are unique to a country, this guidance note's application will need to be adapted to the contexts specific to the country and sector.[2]

B.   Context

This guidance note is an accompanying material of the SARD's GESI framework, which guides the operationalization of the mandates of the first two operational priorities of ADB's Strategy 2030 in South Asia (box).[3] Specifically, this note supports the fourth key area of action of the GESI framework: "Strengthening systems, tools, and competencies of ADB staff and consultants, and agencies and contractors."[4] For definitions and understanding of key GESI concepts and the description of the three pillars of the analytical framework used in this guidance note—(i) understand for action, (ii) empower for change, and (iii) include for opportunity—please refer to the SARD GESI framework (footnote 4).

---

[1]   For the purpose of this note, the term "sector agency" refers to a government ministry, department, or agency, which is mandated to manage a specific sector of public administration. It can be the whole government structure for the sector (e.g., a ministry) or one organ of the structure (e.g., a department). For example, the GESI operational guidelines of the Government of Nepal's Ministry of Physical Infrastructure and Transport and its Ministry of Urban Development provided directives for addressing GESI across the full government structures. Government of Nepal, Ministry of Physical Infrastructure and Transport. 2017. *Gender Equality and Social Inclusion Operational Guidelines 2017*. Kathmandu; and Government of Nepal, Ministry of Urban Development. 2013. *Gender Equality and Social Inclusion (GESI) Operational Guidelines, 2013*. Kathmandu.

[2]   This guidance note should be used to complement any other core guidance notes, including gender guidelines and tip sheets issued by ADB's Strategy, Policy, and Partnerships Department and its Climate Change and Sustainable Development Department.

[3]   This guidance note aims to facilitate the implementation of the SARD's GESI framework, which (i) includes diverse sexual orientation, gender identity and expression, and sex characteristics (SOGIESC) among the identified dimensions of inequality and exclusion in South Asia; and (ii) promotes the empowerment and inclusion of people with diverse SOGIESC. However, it advises users to observe safe and appropriate, or ethical ways in applying it in countries that do not legally recognize people with diverse SOGIESC and have laws that punish their identities and same-sex sexual activities. Any actions (including data collection) covered by this guidance note should do no harm to anyone, especially disadvantaged groups. In countries where people with diverse SOGIESC are legally recognized (Bhutan, India, and Nepal) and transgender people are supported by government policies and programs (Bangladesh), this guidance note urges their engagement—with representation across the SOGIESC or lesbian, gay, bisexual, transgender, queer, and intersex community—in the formulation of the GESI strategy. "People with diverse SOGIESC" refers to those whose sexual orientation, gender identity, expression, or sex characteristics are outside of the binary gender and sex categories. M.V.L. Badgett and R. Sell. 2018. *A Set of Proposed Indicators for the LGBTI Inclusion Index*. New York: United Nations Development Programme.

[4]   ADB. Forthcoming. *Framework for Integrating Gender Equality and Social Inclusion in ADB South Asia Department Operations*. Manila. The fourth key areas of action is illustrated in Figure 2.4 and explained in para. 14 (iv). This guidance note should be read with the framework.

Box: Operational Priorities of the South Asia Department

- **Operational priority 1** is "addressing remaining poverty and reducing inequalities," whereby the Asian Development Bank commits to supporting human development and social inclusion.
- **Operational priority 2** is "accelerating progress in gender equality," whereby the Asian Development Bank commits to support targeted operations to empower women and girls and mainstream gender to narrow gender gaps.

Source: Asian Development Bank. 2018. *Strategy 2030: Achieving a Prosperous, Inclusive, Resilient, and Sustainable Asia and the Pacific.* Manila.

C. Target Audience

This guidance note is for government sector agencies (sector ministries, departments, and/or other relevant bodies) and ADB-supported projects' executing agencies and implementing agencies[5] in South Asia that seek ADB's assistance in developing a strategy for mainstreaming GESI in their organizations, programs, and projects. The target audience includes ADB SARD staff (project teams and GESI teams at the ADB headquarters and resident missions) assigned to assist ADB's partner agencies in developing a GESI strategy.

D. Rationale for Developing a Gender Equality and Social Inclusion Strategy of a Sector Agency

A GESI strategy (i) helps ensure that the sector agency adopts a GESI-responsive approach to improve women's and excluded and vulnerable groups' access to sector resources, opportunities, and benefits; and (ii) increases these groups' visibility in the sector agencies' structures (including leadership and decision-making bodies). A GESI strategy for a sector agency will help ensure that

(i)   sector policies, institutions, programs, and projects implemented by the sector agency promote GESI;
(ii)   projects and activities of the sector agency identify and reduce existing gender and social inequalities and undo the mechanisms that caused them; and
(iii) the sector agency instills a sense of accountability for GESI at all levels of the organization and shows ways to make a midcourse correction in case of deviation.

In line with its GESI framework, SARD will assist the sector agencies in developing a GESI strategy that covers all three pillars of the leave-no-one-behind framework of the former Department for International Development of the United Kingdom:[6] (i) understand for action, (ii) empower for change, and (iii) include for opportunity.[7] This note details the practical steps for developing a sector agency's GESI strategy along these three pillars.

---

[5]   The executing agency, as identified in a financing agreement or technical assistance agreement, is responsible for carrying out a loan, grant, or a technical assistance grant-funded project. The executing agency designates an implementing agency to implement the project and recruit consultants.
[6]   The Department for International Development is now the Foreign, Commonwealth and Development Office.
[7]   The SARD GESI framework (footnote 4) explains the three pillars of the GESI analytical framework.

CHAPTER 2

Developing GESI Strategy of a Sector Agency

A. Defining a Gender Equality and Social Inclusion Strategy and Its Key Elements

A GESI strategy of a sector agency requires integrating GESI considerations in the agency's operations and management. This includes integrating GESI into the agency's policy directives, institutional arrangements, programming, budgeting, project life cycle, and monitoring and evaluation (M&E) systems, which should begin with assessing their provisions that promote or constrain the elimination of barriers to GESI experienced by women and excluded and vulnerable groups. Overall, the formulation and implementation of the GESI strategy will depend on the national and state or local GESI laws that the agency is legally required to observe. This includes laws governing the following:

(i) **External operations.** These include ensuring equality of access to the services of the sector agency, especially of women and disadvantaged groups; collecting disaggregated data by sex or gender and social indicators on beneficiaries and including these data in sector agency reports; forming (e.g., electricity, water, transport) user committees with significant representation of women and disadvantaged groups in the management; and other such policy provisions.

(ii) **Internal operations.** These include maternity leave and paternity leave or parental leave; provision of childcare and a breastfeeding room; gender-segregated toilets for women and men and gender-inclusive toilets for transgender people and others who identify outside the gender binary categories; occupational health and safety standards; promotion of equality in recruitment, promotion, and career development opportunities; and anti-sexual harassment mechanisms, which are covered under institutional analysis.

(iii) **Other factors that facilitate gender equality and social inclusion integration.** These include allocating a GESI-responsive budget, preparing a gender or GESI action plan, assigning or forming GESI focal points or teams or GESI budget cells, and conducting a social and gender audit of programs and projects of the sector agency.

B. Planning for the Development of a Gender Equality and Social Inclusion Strategy

A well-informed GESI strategy for a sector agency is based on a thorough understanding of existing capacities, situations, opportunities, and challenges disadvantaged groups face in accessing the benefits of the agency's projects and programs, and the strengths and weaknesses of the sector agency itself. This responds to the "understand for action" pillar of the GESI analytical framework.

C.   Assessment of the Existing Gender Equality and Social Inclusion Situation

It is important to conduct two assessments that should inform the GESI strategy:

(i)   An in-depth assessment of the situation of women and other disadvantaged groups to understand the barriers and root causes limiting women and other excluded and vulnerable people from enjoying the full benefits of sector projects. Women's disproportionate burden of unpaid care household work may be one such barrier in all countries in the region. This assessment should include the role that men and masculinity play in imposing barriers on women and other disadvantaged groups, including men of disadvantaged groups. The results can improve the sector agency's understanding of and services for women and disadvantaged groups.

(ii)   An in-depth analysis of country-specific sector commitments for the project's target beneficiary groups and identification of key government agencies mandated to work for each category. The analysis is conducted at five operational levels according to the analytical framework: (a) sector policy analysis, (b) sector institutional analysis, (c) sector programming and budgeting analysis, (d) sector reporting, and (e) M&E analysis.

The overall process of conducting these assessments is similar to the GESI assessment for ADB's country partnership strategies and project design features. For detailed guidance on planning the above assessments and developing checklists of relevant questions, data collection, compilation, analysis, and validation, refer to the SARD GESI framework's guidance note for conducting GESI analysis.[8]

D.   Participatory Process for Strategy Development

The formulation of the GESI strategy of a sector agency will greatly benefit from an inclusive and participatory approach with the engagement of different stakeholders, including women, men, disadvantaged groups, and those representing them, like civil society organizations. This process may take different forms, either in-depth with continuous involvement of representatives of civil society organizations—especially organizations of disadvantaged groups and their support nongovernment organizations—or a few consultations with specific interest groups. Table 1 provides guides for the participatory development of the GESI strategy (Appendix 1 provides an indicative outline of the GESI strategy document).

---

[8]   ADB. Forthcoming. *Gender Equality and Social Inclusion Analysis to Inform ADB's Country Partnership Strategies and Project Designs in South Asia: A Guidance Note.* Manila.

Table 1: Tips for Adopting a Participatory Process for Developing a Gender Equality and Social Inclusion Strategy

Stage	Tips to Using a Participatory Process
Inception	1. Form a task force comprising members from the sector government ministry, departments, and other relevant government stakeholders. The key responsibility of the task force is to provide policy and process guidance for strategy development. 2. Form a representative working committee with 5–6 persons from this task force, which can work closely with the strategy development consultant and staff member to ensure contents are relevant for the sector and GESI. 3. If considered appropriate by the sector agency, invite representatives of civil society organizations and specific interest groups working in the sector as task force members to provide insights into the design of the strategy development process.[a] 4. Orient the task force and working committee on GESI concepts and processes.
Strategy development planning	1. Develop a strategy development plan with the working committee, including meetings with key informants, workshops with key stakeholders at different levels, and focus group discussions with members from excluded and vulnerable groups to gather their insights and suggestions on the strategy content. Refer to footnote 3 of the main text for guidance on inviting representatives from the diverse SOGIESC community. 2. Develop a ToC for the strategy on GESI (Appendix 2). 3. Develop a table of contents (based on a government-approved strategy outline) with the working committee for the strategy document. 4. Validate the strategy development plan, ToC, and table of contents with the task force.
Data collection	1. Develop instruments and tools for collecting data disaggregated by sex or gender and other social categories (various excluded and vulnerable groups) to assess and improve the sector agency's understanding of and services for the disadvantaged groups. 2. Collect data using different methods and tools as relevant, e.g., document review, meetings, consultations, workshops, and focus group discussions.[a] 3. Formulate gender- and social identity-differentiated labor, access, and control profiles to increase familiarity with the existing gender and social relations in the sector.
Data processing	1. Compile, process, and analyze collected data and information, and present to stakeholders (including women, men, and disadvantaged groups) and their organizations for validation. 2. Prepare subsections of the draft strategy document and regularly share them with the working committee in an iterative process.
Validation and strategy finalization	1. Prepare a draft GESI strategy with the support of a GESI expert (consultant or staff) and share it with the task force for feedback or input. 2. Share the GESI strategy in consultation meetings with stakeholder groups and finalize it based on their comments and input.[a] 3. Develop a logical framework as part of the strategy (Appendix 3).

GESI = gender equality and social inclusion; SOGIESC = sexual orientation, gender identity and expressions, and sex characteristics; ToC = theory of change.

[a] Refer to footnote 3 of the main text for guidance on inviting representatives from the diverse SOGIESC community.

Source: Asian Development Bank (South Asia Department).

E. Developing the Sector Agency's Institutional Gender Equality and Social Inclusion Policies

The GESI strategy of the sector agency must be supported by an institutional GESI policy that mandates the agency to respond to the barriers to GESI faced by women and disadvantaged groups, and to develop and adopt a GESI strategy. A GESI policy recognizes the following:

(i)   The abilities and constraints experienced by women and excluded and vulnerable people to access and use the resources and/or services of the sector agency.

(ii)   The various factors that constrain them from accessing the sector's resources and services, including the impact of gender (including the role of men and masculinity); income; caste/ethnicity; religion; sexual orientation, gender identity and expression, and sex characteristics (SOGIESC); and geographic location on women and excluded and vulnerable groups.

(iii) Participatory approaches to promote women's and excluded and vulnerable groups' access to and use of the sector's resources and services.

(iv)   The skills and capacities of women, men, girls, boys, people with diverse SOGIESC, and excluded and vulnerable groups as change agents (not mere beneficiaries), and the need to protect and promote their rights.

The GESI policy could be linked to a national law on GESI that is relevant to the sector and should have specific provisions related to the agency's purpose, e.g., to strengthen the education or health services or employable skills of women, people with disabilities, or disadvantaged social identity groups (responding to the "empower for change" pillar of the GESI analytical framework). It will also be essential for the GESI policy to create context-specific enabling environments by including (i) legal reforms to change discriminatory policies and policy provisions regarding the participation of women and disadvantaged groups in decision-making forums, and (ii) a structural change in access to resources and opportunities (responding to the "include for opportunity" pillar of the analytical framework). The GESI strategy document will begin with a presentation of this overall institutional GESI policy of the agency.

Apart from the overall institutional sector agency GESI policy, GESI also needs to be integrated into the other policies of the sector agency. The process of integrating GESI into these policies will be a key component of the GESI strategy. Key policies for GESI mainstreaming are (i) a vision, mission, and values statement; (ii) an organizational and project development cycle (e.g., situational analysis, planning and budgeting, and M&E); (iii) human resource management (e.g., selection and recruitment, training, career promotion, work-life balance programs, worker or staff relations); (iv) financial and administrative management; and (v) operations manual. Table 2 provides guidance (aligned with the three pillars of the leave-no-one-behind framework or SARD's GESI analytical framework) for integrating GESI into the sector agency's policies.

F.   Developing Gender Equality and Social Inclusion-Responsive Institutional Arrangements

Another critical component of the GESI strategy is the institutional structure designed to lead and facilitate GESI mainstreaming at all levels of the sector agency, covering the ministry and department(s) at the national level and implementation structure at the subnational levels. Measures to design the institutional arrangements include strengthening the capacity of existing human resources on GESI through (i) basic orientation on GESI for all staff (as everyone—with or without explicit roles in implementing the GESI action plan—has a role to play in making the organization an enabling environment for GESI); (ii) advanced and skills-based training for senior policy makers, unit managers (e.g., for planning, M&E, human resource management, administrative management), project managers, and GESI focal persons or teams; (iii) specification of the location of GESI responsibility at the national and subnational levels; (iv) promotion of staff diversity that reflects GESI principles; and (v) GESI-responsive human resource policies.

Table 2: Guidance on Integrating Gender Equality and Social Inclusion in Policies of the Sector Agencies

GESI Analytical Framework Pillar(s)	Task	Guidance
Understand for action	Policy development	Adequately address GESI issues in the concept note or terms of reference for the development or amendment of any policy. Also, include them in the policy's objectives and scope of work and tasks.
	Policy formulation team	Include a GESI expert knowledgeable in local realities on the policy development team. Conduct a basic orientation on GESI concepts for all team members.
	Literature review	Review related literature on GESI issues, good practices, and lessons learned to assess and improve the sector agency's understanding of and services for women and disadvantaged groups.
Empower for change, include for opportunity	Policy formulation process	Hold consultations with (i) women and disadvantaged groups to understand their perspectives and priorities, (ii) GESI experts (such as representatives of women's rights organizations) to ensure that all GESI-related issues are well covered, (iii) key sector informants for insights regarding the GESI aspects of the sector, and (iv) responsible government officials in the sector agency.
	Contents of policy documents	1. Clearly define target disadvantaged groups. 2. Specify the reason for formulating the policy and give disaggregated data on the situation of women and disadvantaged groups in the context and situational analysis section. 3. Describe the barriers women and disadvantaged groups experience in accessing and using the agency's services as challenges. 4. Present the agency's responses to the challenges and opportunities and approaches to achieve GESI. 5. Review who will benefit from the policy (gender, social identity, SOGIESC community, class, location, ethnicity disaggregation).

GESI = gender equality and social inclusion; SOGIESC = sexual orientation, gender identity and expressions, and sex characteristics.
Source: Adapted from Government of Nepal, Ministry of Physical Infrastructure and Transport. 2017. *Gender Equality and Social Inclusion Operational Guidelines 2017.* Kathmandu; and Government of Nepal, Ministry of Urban Development. 2013. *Gender Equality and Social Inclusion (GESI) Operational Guidelines, 2013.* Kathmandu (developed with the support of the Nepal Resident Mission of the Asian Development Bank).

A common understanding of the GESI objectives and plan of the sector agency needs to be developed at all institutional levels through regular capacity enhancement of staff, managers, leaders, and directors at all levels. All such measures will contribute to making the organization more inclusive and contribute to changing discriminatory policies and practices in line with the "include for opportunity" pillar of the analytical framework. Managers and staff at different levels of a sector agency will be responsible for implementing the new GESI strategy once approved. Table 3 provides guidance on making the institutional arrangements of sector agencies gender and socially inclusive.

Table 3: Guidance on Developing Institutional Arrangements for Gender Equality and Social Inclusion

Institutional Arrangements	Guidance
GESI responsibility in the sector agency offices	**GESI section or unit.** Declare/designate a specific unit (e.g., GESI unit, social unit) as the GESI specialist section. It will be responsible for providing technical support on GESI to the sector agency and for monitoring and reporting on the implementation of the agency's GESI strategy. Locate this unit in the organizational structure of the agency.
GESI in regular functions of sector agency offices	1. **Recruitment, promotion, transfer.** Follow affirmative action or positive discrimination (giving more attention to excluded people) as far as possible during staff recruitment and promote staff diversity at each level. Include GESI-sensitive criteria for posting and transfer of staff (e.g., considering spousal location; career development of women staff; a lower number of years of experience for internal promotion of women, people with disabilities, people from the transgender communities, and/or any community experiencing historical disadvantage). 2. **Support for gender equality in performance.** To institutionalize the participation of women and other disadvantaged groups in the sector agency's offices, clearly institute and communicate additional arrangements, e.g., facilities for childcare, breastfeeding time and flexible family-friendly work schedule, disability-friendly infrastructure, and an inclusive work environment for people with diverse sexual orientation, gender identity and expressions, and sex characteristics (SOGIESC). 3. **Grievance redress mechanisms.** In consultation with staff, develop grievance redress mechanisms for handling sexual harassment and language-, culture-, or caste-based discrimination issues. Create safe spaces or mechanisms, support groups, or point persons (e.g., ombudspersons) within the sector and organizations at various levels for airing and addressing grievances. 4. **Create an appropriate work culture.** There should be zero tolerance of any discriminatory behavior in language or gestures or other forms. Promote a positive and safe environment that appreciates the perspectives of a diverse group of staff. 5. **Terms of reference.** Job descriptions and terms of reference should include GESI-related tasks in assignment-related objectives, responsibilities, and required qualifications or skills. 6. **Capacity development.** Plan and implement strategies to enhance capacities and skills in mainstreaming GESI. Establish quotas for women and other disadvantaged groups in training and exposures to areas with training-related best practices. 7. **Staff performance evaluation.** Include an evaluation of efforts to address GESI-related issues and GESI-sensitive behavior and actions in staff performance evaluation. Ensure all staff are made accountable for the actions needed to implement the GESI strategy.

GESI = gender equality and social inclusion.

Note: For further information on how to make the workplace inclusive of people with diverse SOGIESC: N. Nambiar and P. Shahani. 2018. *A Manifesto of Trans Inclusion in the Indian Workplace.* Mumbai: Godrej India Culture Lab.

Source: Adapted from Government of Nepal, Ministry of Physical Infrastructure and Transport. 2017. *Gender Equality and Social Inclusion Operational Guidelines 2017.* Kathmandu; and Government of Nepal, Ministry of Urban Development. 2013. *Gender Equality and Social Inclusion (GESI) Operational Guidelines, 2013.* Kathmandu (developed with the support of the Nepal Resident Mission of the Asian Development Bank).

G.   Budgeting for Gender Equality and Social Inclusion in Sector Agencies

Sufficient budgetary allocations must be made to mainstream GESI in operations and management of the sector agency in line with the "include for opportunity" pillar of the GESI analytical framework. The guides for addressing GESI issues in budgeting are provided in Table 4.

Table 4: Guidance on Budgeting for Gender Equality and Social Inclusion in Sectoral Agencies

Budgeting Area	Guidance
Allocation of a GESI budget for different units and departments of the agency	1. Direct the different subdivisions within the sector agency to ensure GESI aspects are integrated into the annual program and allocate an adequate budget for their effective implementation. 2. While preparing directives and budget allocations to all levels of the sector agency, provide direction about the following: (i) the necessity of allocating sufficient budget for GESI assessments (e.g., to identify and analyze the situation of women and disadvantaged groups in covered areas) and developing a GESI action plan to respond to the assessment results, including providing services to reach underserved areas and communities; and (ii) budget for developing capacities (a) to mainstream GESI in the sector agency, including at the ministry and the subnational and local levels, and (b) to monitor and evaluate the GESI results.
Allocation of project budget	Budget allocation for specific projects should cover activities representing all three pillars of the GESI analytical framework: (i) "understand for action," which is the analysis of the barriers to GESI experienced by women and excluded and vulnerable groups and their capacity to promote GESI; (ii) "empower for change," which is the promotion of the livelihood, voice, and social empowerment of women and excluded and vulnerable groups; and (iii) "include for opportunity," which is the ensuring of the GESI-responsiveness of the social, political, and physical environment, including infrastructures, technologies, resources, and services.[a]

GESI = gender equality and social inclusion.
[a] Refer to the South Asia Department's GESI framework for further explanation of the three pillars of the GESI analytical framework.
Source: Asian Development Bank (South Asia Department).

H.   Developing and Implementing Gender Equality and Social Inclusion in Sector Projects

GESI considerations must be mainstreamed throughout the life cycle of the agency's projects. Table 5 provides guidance on integrating and implementing GESI in sector projects following the three GESI analytical framework pillars.

**Table 5: Guidance on Integrating and Implementing Gender Equality
and Social Inclusion in Projects**

GESI Pillar	Project Stage	Guidance
Understand for Action	Project identification	1. Carry out studies, dialogues, or consultations to identify the barriers and capacities of women and disadvantaged groups and the measures required to address GESI. 2. Identify existing disadvantaged groups and their situations through extensive community and stakeholder consultations in the project area, recognizing intersectional inequalities. The data and evidence from the previous situational and policy assessments should inform these project-specific consultations. 3. Identify all possible steps to be taken or provisions to be made by the sector agency to mitigate constraints and barriers that are likely to be experienced by women and excluded and vulnerable groups. 4. Include in the project design the preparation of appropriate communication plans, awareness generation campaigns, and social and other mass media activities.
	Needs assessment	1. Conduct a project-specific situational assessment to identify the needs of women and other disadvantaged groups in the project area to inform the project preparation team about their current situation, including dominant social norms. Ensure participation of these groups in needs assessment, disaggregated by gender and other social groups including disability; age; SOGIESC; and social identity (caste, ethnicity, and religion). 2. Use appropriate tools, such as social mapping, public hearings, and focus group discussions, to assess the needs of women and disadvantaged groups.
	Project preparation	Conduct detailed feasibility studies and on-site appraisals of financial, technical, economic, and institutional aspects, identifying the requirements to empower women and disadvantaged groups and shift discriminatory policies and practices.
Empower for change, include for opportunity	Project appraisal	1. Critically review the studies, options considered, and recommendations of the project preparation team for the project's GESI features before the project is approved for funding. 2. Project appraisal criteria should evaluate the degree to which GESI issues are identified in the proposed project, the level of involvement of women and disadvantaged groups, and how well the project design addresses their barriers and strengthens their empowerment and shifts in discriminatory practices.
	Project implementation	Integrate GESI aspects in all stages of project implementation 1. Ensure the full implementation of the project's GESI design features. 2. Ensure that budgetary allocations for GESI-specific and supportive activities are used efficiently and effectively. 3. Identify and address problems or obstacles to implementing the project's GESI activities and achieving targeted GESI results.
	Reporting, monitoring, and evaluation of project activities	1. Develop GESI outcome and output indicators to measure or describe the project's GESI results; design reporting formats, monitoring processes, and criteria to report the progress and results of GESI activities. 2. Collect and analyze project data disaggregated by sex or gender and other relevant variables, such as age, disability, SOGIESC, social identity (ethnic group or caste), geographic location, and poverty, and conduct case studies of the types of benefits women, men, and people with diverse SOGIESC of disadvantaged groups derive from the project. 3. Regularly monitor and evaluate the project's GESI activities and results and include the results in the project's and agency's reports. In addition, encourage independent benefits monitoring and evaluation by third parties.

continued on next page

Table 5 *continued*

GESI Pillar	Project Stage	Guidance
		4. Submit reports on benefits monitoring and evaluation findings to the relevant management authorities on time. This will help project managers and planners to identify areas where the GESI aspects of the project design can be further improved to achieve its desired objectives and to use this information to better design future projects.
		5. Provide incentives and/or awards for the projects that have addressed GESI successfully.

GESI = gender equality and social inclusion; SOGIESC = sexual orientation, gender identity and expression, and sex characteristics.

Source: Adapted from Government of Nepal, Ministry of Physical Infrastructure and Transport. 2017. *Gender Equality and Social Inclusion Operational Guidelines 2017*. Kathmandu; and Government of Nepal, Ministry of Urban Development. 2013. *Gender Equality and Social Inclusion (GESI) Operational Guidelines, 2013*. Kathmandu (developed with the support of the Nepal Resident Mission of the Asian Development Bank).

I. Strengthening the Gender Equality and Social Inclusion Monitoring and Evaluation System

The sector agency's existing M&E systems should cover GESI performance indicators of targeted outcomes and outputs as listed in the GESI theory of change or design and monitoring framework (logical framework). The progress made on GESI-related performance indicators is to be part of the regular monitoring and reporting process and presented in a subsection of the annual report. Additionally, the reporting on data disaggregated by sex or gender, age, disability, SOGIESC, social identity (ethnic groups or castes), geographic location, and income status is scheduled at frequent and regular intervals.

Regular systems and processes operated and managed by skilled staff are required to develop and strengthen the sector agency's systems and procedures for each phase of the organizational and project development cycle, including analysis, planning, implementation, and M&E. Table 6 provides guidance on integrating GESI into the existing M&E and reporting systems of the sector agency, including monitoring the implementation of the GESI strategy.

Table 6: Guidance on Gender Equality and Social Inclusion Integration in Existing Monitoring, Evaluation, and Reporting Systems

Task	Guidance
Monitoring	1. Ensure that GESI indicators developed during project design are included in the sector agency's internal monitoring and evaluation mechanism, processes, and formats. Include GESI indicators on the quality of services to women and disadvantaged groups. 2. Assess whether women and excluded and vulnerable groups have benefited or not from the programs and projects, and how to improve their access to program and project resources and benefits of the projects or programs. 3. Ensure the ministry's plan covers the outcome indicators, the ways to measure or assess these indicators, and the level of data disaggregation identified during the project design phase. 4. Establish monitoring and evaluation systems with the participation of stakeholder groups (e.g., involved government agencies and business organizations, beneficiary organization, and other civil society organizations). 5. Promote joint monitoring with local stakeholders and target beneficiary groups. 6. Collect disaggregated data and evidence on issues affecting women and excluded and vulnerable groups to inform decisions.
Reporting	1. Include GESI dimensions in reporting formats. 2. Include disaggregated data on beneficiary households in reporting progress against GESI outcome and output indicators. 3. Prepare comparisons of the relevant outcome indicators for different social groups over time. 4. Include good practices, challenges, lessons learned, and suggestions from a GESI perspective in reports. 5. Prepare case studies that reflect women's and excluded and vulnerable groups' stories about their level of benefits from the project to identify good practices and lessons.
Evaluation	1. Include GESI as a key responsibility in the terms of reference of evaluation studies. 2. Include a GESI expert in the evaluation team. 3. Use both quantitative and qualitative evaluation methods. 4. Include clear documentation of the implications and impacts on women and disadvantaged groups.

GESI = gender equality and social inclusion.

The monitoring of the implementation of the GESI strategy should:
1. Be conducted by the GESI unit.
2. Be integrated into the regular monitoring process of the sector agency.
3. Be evaluated by a third-party.

Source: Asian Development Bank (South Asia Department).

APPENDIXES

Appendix 1: Indicative Outline for Gender Equality and Social Inclusion Strategy Documents

Chapter	Key Contents
Introduction	1. Context (e.g., links with national laws, sectoral guidelines, and institutional policies to promote GESI) 2. Rationale for the sector GESI strategy 3. Objectives (e.g., GESI-responsive approach adopted to ensure women's and disadvantaged groups' access to and use of sector resources and benefits; GESI mainstreamed in sector programming and institutions) 4. Definitions (e.g., key concepts like gender equality, women's empowerment, social inclusion, masculinity, SOGIESC, and intersectionality) 5. Key principles and core requirements for addressing GESI (e.g., management commitment to embed GESI as relevant in different aspects of programming, basic understanding of GESI concepts of staff, allocation of time to staff to work on GESI aspects, disaggregation of data) 6. Methodology (e.g., participatory and inclusive approach; consultations with different stakeholders, including women and excluded and vulnerable groups)
GESI assessment of the sector	GESI profile of the sector: 1. Barriers to GESI, trends, challenges, and opportunities 2. Stakeholder analysis (internal and external stakeholders)
Sector agency's GESI strategy	Agency policies and tools to implement national GESI laws, sector guidelines, and institutional response to GESI issues and concerns in the sector and agency: 1. GESI in the sector agency's vision, mission, and values statement; GESI in the sector agency's theory of change 2. **Internal operations.** Examples include human resource management (e.g., recruitment and selection, rewards and incentives, training, career promotion, worker or staff relations, anti-sexual harassment mechanisms, grievance redress mechanisms); work-life balance (maternity leave and paternity leave, provision of child daycare and breastfeeding rooms, family support programs); quotas aimed at increasing representation of women and disadvantaged groups in decision-making bodies; gender-disaggregated toilets; occupational health and safety standards; finance management (including GESI budget); GESI in the project development cycle (GESI-responsive planning and budgeting, implementation, and monitoring and evaluation), including the preparation, implementation, and monitoring and evaluation of a gender or GESI action plan; and assignment or formation of a gender focal point or gender budget cell 3. **External operations.** Examples include developing an operations manual that spells out procedures to ensure equality of access to the services of the sector agency, especially for women and disadvantaged groups; collecting and analyzing data on sector agency beneficiaries disaggregated by sex or gender and social indicators, and including these data in sector agency reports; engaging communities through the formation of service (electricity, water, transport) user committees with significant representation of women and disadvantaged groups and forming networks promoting GESI in the sector
Institutional arrangements for GESI mainstreaming	Tools, measures, guidelines, and strategies for the following: 1. Strengthening the capacity and understanding of staff on GESI concepts and skills 2. Locating responsibility from national to subnational levels for GESI (e.g., the tasks of divisions, departments, and sections to mainstream GESI in the sector ministry, line agencies, and government offices at subnational levels) 3. Promotion of staff diversity 4. Ensuring a common understanding of GESI objectives and strategies at national and subnational levels. 5. Identify responsible units and people for the implementation of the GESI strategy of the sector agency

GESI = gender equality and social inclusion; SOGIESC = sexual orientation, gender identity and expression, and sex characteristics.

Source: Asian Development Bank (South Asian Department).

Appendix 2: Guide for Developing a Theory of Change for the Sector Gender Equality and Social Inclusion Strategy

Step	Guidance
Define the problem and gather evidence	1. Present the objective(s) of the GESI strategy and the target audience. 2. Develop the ToC based on a clear statement of the GESI problem and how it will be overcome by the project interventions. 3. Review existing evidence and data (disaggregated) related to the problem and other projects with similar objectives. 4. Supplement the review with field research and consultations with relevant stakeholders, including women and men and people of disadvantaged groups in the communities, as required. 5. Summarize the state of knowledge on the subject and identify the program's expected GESI outcomes (based on theory or empirical studies). 6. Work backward through components of the ToC, adopting a participatory process involving input and feedback from staff members and stakeholders.
Define the intended outcomes	Develop a set of GESI outcomes drawing on the analysis of the problem and evidence from the literature review or field research. Include in the definition of outcomes if counterfactual evaluation is required to measure outcomes.
Identify program outputs	1. Identify program outputs required for the expected outcomes. 2. Consult stakeholders and review evidence to link the theoretical framework with practical context. 3. Expand assumptions to connect the things the organization can control (outputs) with the changes they should produce that are outside of the organization's control (outcomes). 4. Define GESI-related outputs that are specific and measurable and can be tracked through monitoring.
Define program activities	1. Choose activities that can address the analytical domains of change of the South Asia Department GESI framework (understand, empower, and include) and contribute to the pillars of operational priorities 1 and 2. 2. Specify GESI program activities that can be tracked through activity monitoring with disaggregation (as required).
Map pathways between components	1. Reaffirm the logic of the identified activities, outputs, and outcomes. Identify additional activities to address any gaps, if any. 2. Ensure that livelihood and voice empowerment of women and disadvantaged groups and discriminatory policies and mindsets are addressed throughout the ToC.
Identify assumptions	For each link between activity and GESI output, and GESI output and GESI outcome, identify assumptions that must hold if the program is to work as expected.
Identify risks	To identify risks, ask the following questions: 1. What are the forces acting against project success? 2. What occurrences or actions might happen at any point in the project cycle that would significantly jeopardize the achievement of the intended results? 3. Link each risk to a specific output. 4. Do not include as risks (i) any factors that the project fully controls, (ii) risks already eliminated through redesign, and (iii) planned mitigation measures. 5. For all projects and operations, list all project risks in the risk assessment and prepare a risk management plan. 6. List mitigating measures for each identified risk in the risk management report.

GESI = gender equality and social inclusion, ToC = theory of change.

Note: A theory of change (ToC) is a method that explains how a given intervention, or set of interventions, is expected to lead to specific development change, drawing on a causal analysis based on available evidence. A good project design is based on an evidence-based ToC developed in consultation with and agreed upon by key stakeholders. A ToC is required for a gender equality and social inclusion strategy to envision the hierarchy of objectives (including outputs and impacts) that the sector agency seeks to achieve and the contributions required to reach the planned objectives. United Nations Development Group. *Theory of Change: UNDAF Companion Guidance.* New York.

Source: Adapted from Government of Nepal, Ministry of Physical Infrastructure and Transport. 2017. *Gender Equality and Social Inclusion Operational Guidelines 2017.* Kathmandu; and Government of Nepal, Ministry of Urban Development. 2013. *Gender Equality and Social Inclusion (GESI) Operational Guidelines, 2013.* Nepal (developed with the support of the Nepal Resident Mission of the Asian Development Bank).

Appendix 3: Guide for Developing a Logical Framework for the Gender Equality and Social Inclusion Strategy of a Sector Agency

Prepare a logical framework for the gender equality and social inclusion (GESI) sector strategy to operationalize the theory of change. Ensure GESI-related aspects are embedded in the results chain of the logical framework. Table A3 provides guidance on formulating GESI-related logical framework components.

Table A3: Guidance on Formulating the Logical Framework for the Gender Equality and Social Inclusion Strategy of a Sector Agency

Results Level	Guidance
Activities and inputs	1. Include activities for the implementation of the strategy 2. Identify the inputs required for the implementation of the GESI strategy
Outputs	Develop outputs related to the implementation of the GESI strategy
Outcomes	Include key GESI outcome statements describing the immediate and direct benefits of achieving the outputs
Impact	Identify the impact of implementing the GESI strategy

GESI = gender equality and social inclusion.

Source: Adapted from Government of Nepal, Ministry of Physical Infrastructure and Transport. 2017. *Gender Equality and Social Inclusion Operational Guidelines 2017*. Kathmandu; and Government of Nepal, Ministry of Urban Development. 2013. *Gender Equality and Social Inclusion (GESI) Operational Guidelines, 2013*. Kathmandu (developed with the support of the Nepal Resident Mission of the Asian Development Bank).

Additionally, make sure that selected performance indicators for the GESI strategy are and GESI responsive as well as specific, measurable, achievable, relevant, and time-bound (SMART):

(i) **Specific.** Details the outputs or outcome the project seeks to achieve by specifying dimensions, such as who, where, when, quality, quantity, and cost.

(ii) **Measurable.** Stated in quantifiable terms (e.g., percentage of people with disabilities) and feasible to collect data in time to report in project progress reports as relevant.

(iii) **Achievable.** Realistic about what is to be achieved. The collective judgment of key stakeholders is needed to choose a target that is ambitious yet realistic.

(iv) **Relevant.** Appropriate to the results statement it measures and useful for management information purposes.

(v) **Time-bound.** Stated with a target and baseline, both with dates.

www.ingramcontent.com/pod-product-compliance
Lightning Source LLC
Chambersburg PA
CBHW042035220326
41599CB00045BA/7470